CW00448891

Copyright © 1989 Colin Robinson
First published 1989 by Blackie and Son Ltd

All rights reserved. No part of this publication may be reproduced,
stored in a retrieval system, or transmitted in any form
or by any means, electronic, mechanical, photocopying, recording
or otherwise without the written permission of the Publishers.

British Library Cataloguing in Publication Data

Robinson, Colin *1950–*
Blackie Bear's tea party.
I. Title
823′.914[J]

ISBN 0-216-92572-X Hbk
ISBN 0-216-92790-0 Pbk

Blackie and Son Ltd
7 Leicester Place
London WC2H 7BP

Printed in Portugal

BLACKIE BEAR'S
Tea Party

Colin Robinson

Blackie

It was a fine spring morning.
   Blackie Bear got up early and made some cakes.
   'I'm going to invite my friends to tea today,' she said.

Blackie Bear carried the cakes outside and
left them to cool down.

'Here you are, birds. There are plenty of
crumbs left for you,' she said.

Just then, Twitch the squirrel scampered past.
'Hey, Twitch, come back here!' shouted
Blackie Bear. 'I want to ask you something.'
But Twitch ran off and hid behind a boulder.

Blackie Bear saw a red tail sticking out from behind the boulder. She tugged it hard.

'Do you mind?' said a big deep voice. It was Bruce the red stag.

'Sssorry,' said Blackie Bear. 'I thought you were Twitch!'

Twitch ran ahead and then dived down
a rabbit hole.
   'Come out, I want to ask you something.'
Blackie Bear called into the hole.
   'Go away,' shouted the angry rabbits.
'You've woken us all up!'

Twitch was enjoying himself. 'You can't catch me!'
he called and darted off, leaping over
some mole hills.

Blackie Bear didn't see them.

'Aaah, somebody stop me!' she cried as she
rolled over and over squashing the mole hills flat.

'You silly, clumsy Bear!' shouted the moles.

Twitch was now racing through a field of sheep.
'Twitch, come back,' shouted Blackie Bear,
running after him.

'Where do you think you're going, disturbing our lambs like that?' said Woolly the sheep crossly.

'Can't stop now,' puffed Blackie Bear and ran on.

Twitch had nearly reached his home on the other side of the river.

'I'll use the stepping stones to get there,' said Blackie Bear.

But Twitch began dropping pine cones onto Blackie Bear's head and she started to wobble.

'Help! I'm slipping . . .' she cried.

SPLOSH! Into the water went Blackie Bear.
  'Quack, quack!' cried the ducks.
'Stupid Bear, you're messing up our nest. Quack!
Quack! Quack!'

'I've had enough of this chasing. I'll leave a
message for Twitch instead,' sighed Blackie Bear.
   As she wandered slowly home, she met the
ducks, Woolly the sheep, the moles, the
rabbits and Bruce the red stag. They were still
very cross with her so she invited them all to tea.

But when Blackie Bear got home
she found that all her cakes had been eaten.
'Now what am I going to do?' she sighed.
A big tear began to roll down her cheek.

Just then, the door opened and in marched
Twitch carrying the biggest bag of nuts that
you ever saw.

Blackie Bear dried her eyes and smiled
a big smile.

Soon the other guests arrived. They all
brought some food so there was plenty to eat.

They talked and laughed until it was dark
outside. Then they left very quietly because
Blackie Bear had fallen asleep!